THE
FIRE
MUSIC

1985

Agnes Lynch Starrett

Poetry Prize

The Fire Music

Liz Rosenberg

University of Pittsburgh Press

Published by the University of Pittsburgh Press, Pittsburgh, Pa. 15260

Feffer and Simons, Inc., London
Manufactured in the United States of America

Library of Congress Cataloging in Publication Data

Rosenberg, Liz.
The fire music.

(Pitt poetry series)
I. Title.
PS3568.07874F57 1986 811′.54 85–40856
ISBN 0-8229-3531-7
ISBN 0-8229-5381-1 (pbk.)

The author and publisher wish to express their grateful acknowledgment to the following publications in which some of these poems first appeared: *The American Poetry Review* ("The Last Word on Eczema"); *Blueline* ("Alone with the Shoe Manufacturer in His Memorial Park"); *Boundary 2* ("The Real True President," "Signs," and "The Speed of Death"); *Crazyhorse* ("Another Sleepless Night Among the Ruins," "First Heat," and "Thanksgiving"); *The Georgia Review* ("What the Trees Suffer"); *Midstream* ("Endless Life," "Laying the Ghosts to Rest," "The Lighthouse," and "Passover"); *The Missouri Review* ("Elegy to a Beagle Mutt" and "Wearing His Old Boots"); *The Nation* ("Into the Territories" and "The Stolen Child"); *New Letters* ("Valentine's Day at Johns Hopkins Hospital"); *The New Republic* ("The One-Legged Boy on the First Day of Spring"); *The Paris Review* ("The Bells of St. Simon" and "A Suburban Childhood"); *Ploughshares* ("At the Common Table" and "Children: 4th of July"); *Prairie Schooner* ("The Accident"); *The Seattle Review* ("Blue Mountain Lake" and "Ghosts"); and *Three Rivers Poetry Review* ("What's in the Air").

"Survival" first appeared in the *Cimarron Review* and is reprinted here with the permission of the Board of Regents for Oklahoma State University, holders of the copyright.

The poems "The Angels Inform the World," "The Christmas Cactus," "Dread," "In the End We Are All Light," "Married Love," and "The Mourner's Christmas" appeared originally in *The New Yorker*.

Some of these poems first appeared in *The Angel Poems* (State Street Press) and in *Apparitions* (Lord John Press).

My thanks to the Pennsylvania Council on the Arts, and to the Kellogg Foundation.

Early on, I had the kind encouragement of Nelson Bentley, Leonard Bernstein, Margaret Hartley, Chip McGram, Howard Moss, and John Gardner. To them all thanks and no blame.

The publication of this book is supported by grants
from the National Endowment for the Arts
in Washington, D.C., a Federal agency,
and the Pennsylvania Council on the Arts.

This book is for John, in memoriam

"i mi ristrinsi alla fida compagna:
e come sare' io sanzi lui corso?
chi m'avria tratto su per la montagna?"

"but I stayed close to my faithful guide:
and how should I have sped without him?
who would have brought me up the mountainside?"

—Dante, *The Purgatorio*

CONTENTS

CONTENTS

I

THE BELLS OF SAINT SIMON

I sail into the crooked gloom
and steer to bed beneath the shining tent
of paint we are experimenting with
and lay this poor drunkard down.
Our town's asleep—
wet wires and frozen glittering domes
under a roof of stars that fishtail out to space.
How many times at this same window have I leaned
to feel the same sheet-lightning crack
when bats revolve at the horizon
and morning slowly rises, plain and blue.

He sleeps like a fallen statue,
dragging a mountain of blankets as he rolls,
his Hebrew hair and beard severely wild.
The sleeping twilight grasshopper folds
her musical bones at morning prayer: delight
dismay colliding as the earth
raises its great sinking heart again
and listens to the shaken clamor of the air.
Five times the church bells break
the violet elements to gold;
three notes a bird calls in reply
as I press both hands against one booming heart;
church music and his breath
pulling like oars against the dark.

CHILDREN: 4th OF JULY

They play ferociously to beat the rain—
my youngest neighbors shrieking in the yard.
"Can you do this?" And Randolph drops
into the dirt. His friend goes wild.
"Can you do this? Can you do *this*?"
she sings, dragging her bony knees along the dust.

Some wise child's chalked in green on the Giant wall,
Don't Eat Stuff Off The Sidewalk.
A music box battle hymn floats out
beyond the bells of the ice-cream truck, where
a black man sits, crestfallen in the street.
He shifts and rises, music hissing from his phones;
on one baroque and twisting skate he glides through dusk.

The ambulance wobbles on its hysterical flute
down Main, past Mickey's Blue Heaven
where customers line up for the display.
One man leans out, his eager hands
outstretched. A woman tilts to his embrace,
her kerchief sloppy over one shut eye.

In the frame of this blissful honeymoon begins this
first extended breath, as the white vein pulses,
cracks and flowers in the deep, overhanging sky.
The lovers watch the war of lights, believing each other
completely
happy as now, between the lunatic blasts, they are.

THE CHRISTMAS CACTUS

All during the Christmas rush
I waited for the thing to come alive.
Eyed it while I gift wrapped scarves,
withered it with scorn as I threw
the green and silver bundles under the tree.
By New Year's
I vowed to be happy
living with just stems.

Then one day in February—
the worst month of the year,
making up in misery what it lacks in length—
the blooms shot out,
three ragged cerise bells that rang
their tardy Hallelujahs on the sill.
Late bloomers,
like the girls that shine
and shine at long last
at the spring dance
from their corner of the gym.

SURVIVAL

Friends come calling
with faces queerly lit, and suffering
far back of the gaze like deer
hot car lights freeze;
green headlamps brilliant in eternity
on winter roads they blow across
drawn down the skittish edge of the universe.

Having read the rags, the *Enquirer* and *Star*
I should die of grief, I should marry
the stricken man whose one communicant
is a psychic squirrel, dancing
on his broken ledge—but my heart goes leaping,
clawing up the blood. The composer waits.
He tilts his head, his gray hair glinting.
The boy delivers a message with his slow way of speaking.
Once more against my will I am escorted
gallantly among the living.

Our gloveless man at K-Mart's entrance
rings his bell, and claps one hand
against a thin gray coat, as shoppers drag home
the burden of their speechless love.
If I ever die, I'll come to stay,
hoping to be some permanent help.
And make my heart a battered gong
and hang it up for birds to hammer;
my bones throw down, that over them
the gall-torn lost may rest their heads.

THE ONE-LEGGED BOY ON THE FIRST DAY OF SPRING

Today an April drizzle
freshens black snow.
I crank the window
to catch a whiff of leaves.
All hell breaks loose,
nostalgia crackles in my chest.
So many springs! I pray,
now let whatever happens come.

Beating his arms like wings,
a boy is hopping down the road—
he flies—playing some game,
getting some place by leaps and bounds.
I slow my car to grin
into his face. His lips
are clenched,
his pale eyes fierce,
the one empty flap of his slacks
whips loose. The drizzle picks up
momentum and slams down.
Life, what do you want?
The kid won't stop, he waves me on.
Head thrown, he gallops.
He drinks down the rain.

BATAVIA, NEW YORK

The old people sit so late into the night
they read by starlight.
They clutch the book straight up
or let it fall a little space upon their chests
as if what was written there still weighed on them.
The underwater spray of t.v.
fills the living room;
blue-gray lightning on the philodendron, on the china dog
asleep in the curio.

At the tip of massive, dreaming oak trees
round green arrows point toward spring.
But the old people, with so much of life behind them
and death ahead, looming like a hill,—
what do they dream?

BLUE MOUNTAIN LAKE

—for my sister

At the edge of Blue Mountain Lake
the smell of pine unfurls like motel soap
we opened in some double room of childhood.
I seem to see you bobbing still, a blue-striped cork
in a phantom, sun-scorched sea—blurring the tow rope
of the water skier, and his white wake,
and the boat which bends and disappears behind a wood.

I whirled, a scarecrow of a child
on my first amusement park ride, New Jersey,
both hands clutching the pinstriped wheel.
You leaned halfway across the world
to tell me, "pass the tea,"
so I did, sliding the make-believe pot to you, eyes wild
till you caught my hands and we both hung on for real.

One day we drove to Coney Island
and you went for a swim.
I let the ocean wet my feet, no more than that,
and kept a watchful eye on your phosphorescent bathing cap
till you reemerged—except, it wasn't you, it was a slim
blonde shaking out her hair. I ran along the sand
crying, till I stumbled on where you sat

staring dead ahead into the water,
dry as a bone.
You guessed the waves were too high, you said.
I only nodded, knees weak with relief,
but I dragged you home
as if you were my only daughter
returned for an evening from the dead.

Now I ask myself, the dutiful student:
How is this blue-capped mountain like you?
You, who are not monumental or stark,

why do you seem to sway at such a height?
You are like the color blue,
that's all. You do not represent
anything, you are simply what you are.

When the strongman's arms begin to break
from holding up the child, and the clock
winds down, I look
into the darkest corner of the nursery.
I find two little girls still playing in the cracks
of light. Their silence makes
a sound like winter snowing in a lake.

A SUBURBAN CHILDHOOD

Having a crush was how I existed—
how I spent recess; I wandered
dull fields gone brilliant
for one sullen boy who strolled scornfully by.
As if in a dream I boarded
strange buses, stepped down
and roamed through the flower-named
streets, past the one house lit up
from within; humming he loves me,
he loves me not yet . .
past mounds of leaves burning
their acid of longing
till in the violet dusk headlights
would splash me; behind them my mother
propped up at the wheel—her mouth open,
the doors of the car flying out—
as she grabbed for me, already screaming.

THE STORY OF MY LIFE

It was my fate to help Billy Redanz learn how to read;
the bully king of second grade, left back three times,
head like a cinder block, with a dirty cowlick
and dirty nails he dug into the book
he pinned between us, torturing each word.

"So the Jews drink children's blood."
His eyes on mine were flat and bright. I drew back,
kicking a line of dirt across his shin,
and dragged him to the principal
who tightened her lipsticked mouth at me,
asked Billy to apologize. I saw in a flash how it was.

He showed up years later, holding a monkey wrench
—muscled, greasy, polite—to fix my father's car.
When I came to the door he grabbed me,
grinning, pressing his lips against my throat.
"So you remember me?" he cried,
"You were so patient, so good, like a little nun."
He kissed my mouth, then off he went with his shining toolbox,
a last touch of his delicate broad fingers in my palm.
All day his cool, his bird-like whistle haunted the driveway,
that old conspiracy of kindness after me again,
another sweetness.

FIRST HEAT

Heat darkens the lamps along the street
as the first lonely attic fan hums on.
I imagine the girl in that cool room, pulling the chain.
Her gold window, finely lit
burns all the grass below.

Around her corner, down the block
some kid is tinkering late in his garage
trying to get just one thing right,
his rolling door left open to a breeze.
Hand tools gleam on the plaster wall
and the way they shine he calls, Oh come to me!
The princess shuts her lamp then, quickly,
lying back down in darkness stretching
her arms up like a fifteenth-century painted saint
shivering, calling Come to me!

WHAT THE TREES SUFFER

Wildflowers, crushed under our feet
hold up their bruised heads in an hour
on queerly broken stems.
Water, wildly beating,
struggles to free itself of stone
bridges and dams; slides like a snake,
silver, crooked and lost among the reeds.
        But the trees suffer most at our hands.
They are almost human, but all are kings
guarding the frail kingdom:
the crown leaves slick with sunlight
as men cast off to sleep
in the dark net below.
In the tale, some careless farmer
taps a sugar maple, then leaves the bucket clinging
to the trunk. Now, years later,
the tree holds out the rusty pail
like a beggar reaching a tin cup
though the cry is "Take! Take!"
Some farmer's child
could slake his thirst for years
on a single icy sip,
would grow to be the prince who knows
the secret of the roots,
if he could find the way.
But all the children's feet
are lost in streams and beds of flowers.

And only the rain comes by—
rattling the leaves, the kingdom's gold,—
and tossing down one by one its miserly dime-thin alms.

TO SPEAK OF THE WOE THAT IS IN MARRIAGE

He sleeps in the gauze-blue, tranquil haze
an hour before dawn, and when I slip out
from the sheets, stand upright
with my bare feet on the freezing floor
in sympathy he heaves onto his side,
dangles his hand out, palm down, like a pope
and from his sleep he murmurs, "Say this one.
The cross between St. Thomas and St. Porter."

Now for a year I've pondered his riddle,
climbing up and down the creaking stairs
with my eyes fixed always on the gold square
of his study window, with my gaze worriedly searching
for his old car with the broken grill out front,
with my heart in my mouth as an old dog gums a bone
each time the phone rings late,
as I will stagger all my life
carrying the doubter's four A.M. terrors,
twisting on my side against the dark waiting
for him to bring the glass of juice
lit like a gem by nightlight;
bearing the bowls of soup, the crackers,
padding the back seat of the car with pillows, blankets,
hauling out the suitcase, maps, the labeled sandwiches.
And when I fall asleep on the velvet sofa
he lifts the whole weight of me in his arms, my legs
brushing against doorknobs, my hair in his mouth,
he staggers as we both fall on the bed.

Powerful, pale sleeper, who brings the blue
back to the daylight-yearning air, who pricks the stars
into their steady evening shining all year long.
Killer of spiders, sorter of moldy goods—

when I look at the vein leaping in his sleeping wrist
I want the fragile world to live forever. I take
from the pulp of many innocent
wind-bearing trees a splinter of the wood
given between St. Thomas and St. Porter,
the spirit of the universe's gift or curse,
which flings out his arm, and presses my feet to this cold spot,
and crosses us together in our love.

THE STOLEN CHILD

Consider the parents of Joey LeDome,
spirited from the county rink
one night in early spring.
By now he is a gangly kid
who shrugs the nickname "Mooch" he skated off with
into darkness, in knit green pants he's long outgrown
which lie discarded in some trailer park,
where he still lives forever
kept to watch t.v. and eat spaghetti from a can.

We think this, studying our quart of milk,
but know, as his parents always knew,
about the razor and the sack
even those weeks they jumped and lurched
on the first blast for his voice on the wire.

They carry it off, Mr. and Mrs. LeDome.
At church, before a curb or elevator
she must dimly glimpse—a gesture, shadow
of a spider's web, some swaying
there, the chance that he
will run back down the park slope
wearing the anxious face of his blurred photograph.
Mr. LeDome mows the grass
relentlessly, and turns under
the fallen leaves or blowing snow like someone
just looking for something he has let get away.

THE LONGING FOR ETERNAL LIFE

Tonight, after a rain
the insects' song comes washing clear
in air worn cool, so thin
I can hear the traffic
lights a block away clicking
and the faintest inclination of car wheels
bending right or left into dim streets.
My porch lamp beams on gourds
swelling by starlight,
groping slowly across the string.

Why is it hard to live like this,
simply to live?
Far off, on a highway dark as ocean water
woodchucks paddle across the road
to pass into eternal life.
I force myself to rest, unfold both fists,
and hear a weary tick-tick-tick—
the ambitious moth
testing her heart against the light.

GHOSTS

Like clockwork, it happens every three, four years,
when he's out alone with some quiet chore—clearing a field
of stones, or calling the wandering cows home;
and though it's happened before and will happen again, he
 believes
at first it's his father, who's been gone these fifteen years,
whose throat is buried deeper than those stones he moves—
or his mother, moving lightly from porch to wet grass in the dark,
calling him to supper, beating the charred kettle like a drum.
And just when he thinks his life is haunted for good
he remembers, and hunts up the source: a wire in the barbed
wire fence or a guy wire holding up the sagging barn—
some bit of steel that's caught the radio waves and plays them
to his farm. And though his throat's as tight as a screw
he laughs, releasing the length of wire fence
he'd come to mend. It's bitten deep into both palms.
Some hamburger ad or love song streams between his hands.
"The damndest thing," he'll later tell his wife,
but he won't say what he thought he heard. And he's glad
to fall for it again next time, to hear those voices
clear as day, live as the ones that call to him at night
in the last blank turning before sleep. He could dream his life
away, he knows, waiting to relive the past again,
but he's not a dreamer, never has been. It takes all he has
to keep the farm alive, the animals safe and warm.

Then one June morning he's startled half out of his wits
by his grandfather's clear "Amen"—religious program, Sunday
 morning—
and a fact from school flies through his head:
that owls send sound waves through their wings

though the sound's too high for human ears.
And he wonders if his animals are haunted, then,
if that's what sends them pushing through the wire fence
to stand bewildered on the other side, dreamily chewing.
And an even stranger thought crosses with his first:
that the deep-eyed owl carries the past
on its back, gliding through the dark-tipped trees
with its burden of all the voices that are, or will be,
or were—ghosts ruffling the gray feathers like wind.

So it isn't a dream he hears, but his own father whistling,
his wife breathing in the dark bed at his side, young, asleep.
And for an instant he half believes his own invention,
listens without meaning to for the blade-sharp floating wing:
no use. The field has fallen into silence, broken
by the summer twittering of a morning sparrow. It's time
to mend the broken fence again, find the lost calves.
And in his own lifted voice, now lashed with tears
he calls the animals home.

THE LIGHTHOUSE

I want to live among the big, bell-like and moving things
with purple beach pea flowers opening
and closing, day into night the beam
casting across the foam.

Summer stars and Roman candles have drowned
themselves hissing down against the black
and gold-lit sea, washing with sailors' caps
at the last thin curve of the Cape, the Light
a pulse of safety when a child
awakens, feels car headlights rake
ceiling and bed, the emptiness of space,

and crosses to the window and looks out.
Then daybreak of the lighthouse swings,
goes steadily across the wall—
a blinking owl at the windowpane,
dragging the mirrored blackness out,
bringing a shining seaweed twig or flowering wave to shore.

I want to live like that,
to be a great and watchful eye
that sends all its light out and takes nothing back.

THE LAST WORD ON ECZEMA

I knew him by his green leather chair,
the thick lenses he wore,
the way he decorously rolled one sleeve
to bare my chafed elbow.
Whadda girl, whadda girl.
He shined his sad lamp on my scales,
snapped off the light in despair.
It made me feel proud,—
survivor of small wars.
I'd driven through strange country,
fields of hay, fields of corn,
mamaloshen of the stick shift singing
in my palm. As he pricked my arm
he murmured, you have to treat from inside,
you with your history.
Hysterical allergies! Allergic
to history! Oh soul of little faith, believe:
there are grandfathers everywhere.
The dead voice rasps in the living ear—
You see this daughter
the one with the rash? A cheater at cards.
Take care of her.

THE ANGELS INFORM THE WORLD

We have all seen them, I think,
heard the garbled messages.
They send us skidding
into snowbanks, inches from poles
that waited woodenly for our final skate
Midnight the clock slickers into place.
What are they doing
by the bed? They hurry away, trailing
a foreign voice and breath.

Night after sodden night we sat awake
in the hospital corridor
on the blue plastic bench, but they never showed.
They must be bewildered by human time.
Even now they are struggling down,
pulled by the stale wind of what we wanted.
They fall on slow ceremonial wings,
nothing in their hands, silk sails tangled,
as we promenade them, sulky and unaware.

DREAD

Every time the door swings shut
a strangled voice sings out, That's it!
Drive slow, I chant
go safe, come home:
our family emblem was disaster.
I jump up to smell his discarded shirt,
already busy planning the funeral.

His brow I've practiced kissing
goodbye—pale, sleeping and narrow,
taking his pulse between my lips.
The sweet flesh tightens, a sinking stone.
My song goes dead,
drones mine, mine, mine.
I learned it at my father's knee,
our house key slung around my neck.

VALENTINE'S DAY
AT JOHNS HOPKINS HOSPITAL

The elevator sinks
to the first floor
where the guard taps his pencil on a wooden desk.
The halls are vacant
though this afternoon we saw mother and child,
both in blue robes, holding hands,
and earlier still the worried crowd
pressing for the doors. Drunks and
nurses, the black man big as a rock
whose bulk was cut off at the hip—
all have gone. In the cafeteria a woman eats
a late meal, rummaging through a paper bag.
There's snow in the yard.

In the yard, the school bus steams.
Late couples take the dark seats
at the back. Snow slides
under the heavy wheels.
Above, the sky's a scratched, smudged yellow.
At each rise
of the wheels, and fall, I'm drawn from you.

Last night the hammock moon slung
light on the rug.
You gathered me up,
your hair like water on my cheek.
Now I walk through snow
that melts on my lips as it falls.
When I left you, you lay
on white sheets,

beautiful, your hands square and hard.
Dogs circle loose in the street,
follow me halfway home, then turn.
I want to go back,
force some burning wish on the stars,
seize you with this mouth, but I do
as you would have me do.
Face my back to the darkness, and walk home.

TRAIN TRAVEL

I wash my hands in someone else's soap,
won't change my socks for fear
my naked feet will make the journey lonelier.
This dented can of Coke comes
from the black-eyed boy in the dining room
who spiked my lunch with arsenic:
at each cold sip my mouth goes numb.
At midnight, in the middle of the country,
inside the crossing of a railroad town
I stare down the darkened tunnel of Main Street.
Two traffic lights blink red and green
like wise, eccentric owls. We're scuttled
along the tracks, under thin tracks of stars
past motel lights and highway streaks. I hear
the long-chorded music of the train horn,
watch our violet lightning jump over on the grass.

And when we come, shaken like laundry
into the air of Los Angeles,
home of the insane, of countless murderers,
a Mexican smiles at me so kindly from his truck
I almost forget the stench—forget the four bitter pennies
I've been clutching in my palm, ashamed
to let the muggers see how fat my wallet is—
and cross in front of him and let my change
fall in the market of forgotten streets,
dropping like bell-notes in the foreign twilight
where even my fear is not worth holding on to.

IN THE END WE ARE ALL LIGHT

I love how old men carry purses for their wives,
those stiff light beige or navy wedge-shaped bags
that match the women's pumps,
with small gold clasps that click open and shut.
The men drowse off in medical center waiting rooms,
with bags perched in their laps like big tame birds
too worn to flap away. Within, the wives slowly undress,
put on the thin white robes, consult, come out
and wake the husbands dreaming openmouthed.

And when they both rise up
to take their constitutional,
walk up and down the block, her arms are free as air,
his right hand dangles down.

So I, desiring to shed this skin
for some light silken one,
will tell my husband, "Here, hold this,"
and watch him amble off into the mall among the shining
cans of motor oil, my leather bag
slung over his massive shoulder bone,
so prettily slender-waisted, so forgiving of the ways
we hold each other down, that watching him
I see how men love women, and women men,
and how the burden of the other comes to be
light as a feather blown, more quickly vanishing.

SIGNS

Face to face with a tilting, rain-worn sign
I stop dead. *Pots* and *post,* I spell obsessively . . . or *opts.*
Smoke moves out across a young man's mouth
as he breathes against an evening breeze.
Walking home, I know what stuff the moon's made of.

Head-deep in berries
I'm thinking pies, while the next row up
a noisy mother instructs her child.
Hear how the berries ping? she asks
as the heavy fruit falls *dock dock dock* into the pail.
That ineluctable woman in her lit house
moves like a kabuki dancer to turn on her blue t.v.
and the plum-colored rose in its round-lipped vase
reads like the symbol of our courteous love
as we touch each other in the dark—lost,—
whispering *here* and *here.*

I've studied the mirror too many long hours,
dreaming like a teenager or lovesick girl
and watched the staring corpse. I can't tell
if it's borning or dying down
but now I'm here, walking
a country road in twilight, breathing the air,
taking the print of Queen Anne's lace on my palm
as a lingering, slow-falling dusk descends.
I'm working to make sense
of sense again, believing secretly
no rusty blood-red lily blooming anywhere will flag me down.

LAYING THE GHOSTS TO REST

—In Memoriam, D. S. F., February 1979

Even the night nurse drowses now
as the bulkhead of midnight moves endlessly through.
The mortal angel slows   slows
at the brooding edge of things.
The stranger sleeping in the next bed turns
her pillow to face a dream, so you turn too
and the soul weighs anchor and slips away.

I did not know
how far the dead could fall.
In the plywood box,
like cargo waiting to be shipped,
you seemed to glare through iron lids,
head grimly tipped,
the skin laid flat against the bone
as if to lock the last old secrets in.

Rabbi Jake Cohen, a perfect stranger,
droned as your spirit rose above the lid,
listened in before it slowly
rolled away, over the tops of the stones, uphill.
Later I could feel you hovering at my ear
as the *yartzeit* candle sputtered
and held still, a thin blue tube.
Be brave, Grandma.

Now that the dust of clouds has rolled you in its waves
I imagine you serve in the hall
of the dead, beneath the moss-green door,
particular about detail, as you were in life,
in the shady Flatbush Avenue home
that soaked up darkness like a sponge.

Silence, desertion, poverty:
what was left you.
And a few old things. The claw-footed armchair,
a pair of lamps—gold angels clinging to the light—
your sofa bed with its filthy cover, twisted stockings
above the tub, no food in the Frigidaire, less and less . . .

Ghosts drift casually through the living room
floating on the turned-off t.v. set.
Visions, flickerings on your white prayer book,
the buzzing of your fly-voice
every time I lift the phone.
Fields of ghosts, their faces livid, their voices snowing
on the black coats of the living,
and the robin plunging by my window
the sound the dog makes behind the door—
I expect them to take on your true form,

shadows fly up under the car wheels,
gathering themselves into a face—
It's you—is it you?
What have you got to tell me?

Last night I woke at three from a bad dream.
I was making the crossing
with Columbus, and he steered us through glowing
upturned bellies of ghostly fish,
peering over the dark rim of the world
to the heart of America.
And all around us, the bodies
were going down. I woke up shouting,

angry, gasping lungs gonging like an iron bell.
Now that I've emptied my hands, Grandma,
now I have nothing, I strike out,
sighting land, losing you.

II

THE REAL TRUE PRESIDENT

Not that sad dreamer, but the one behind the scenes
I want to shake his brass hand,
watch him burst onto the twisting staircase
of America as I have seen him
mornings when he lies grieving over the dead
too heavy to move, thinking how can this go on?
He rolls like a thundercloud across the Midwest
and sets his lightning fork down in the South,
he breaks together the heads of the North and East
and bends over the boiling fountain of the volcano to drink.
I have seen the nations gather round him.
England meets him in the garden secretly,
Russia touches his pocket
and Africa gives him a dark look.
China turns her back and stares covertly at the horizon.
He is the angel of death ascending the ladder toward God
to settle about the immortal soul
with an apologetic excuse and a million complaints;
he believes people are laughing whenever his back is turned.
What has all his strength brought him if he still must contend
with his own mean moods and ugly drunks?
His gold limbs are too heavy to lift
and his jeweled eyes snap shut on a premonition—
this Councilor who can sense his enemies asleep
and knows what they are dreaming,
who hovers over the roofs of the weeping houses,
their sad snows in winter and their short happy summer hours,
who peeks into the lit apartments and sighs
and laughs at the t.v. comedy show laughing hysterically back,

who longs for peace and friendly feeling
and can circle the globe forever
with his loneliness and hunger violently drumming.
He bears it up in darkness and he brings it down in darkness
to the ordinary man of state, that imposter, who lies
sleeping with his troubled gray head resting on a pillow.

ALONE WITH THE SHOE MANUFACTURER IN HIS MEMORIAL PARK

You bang on the statue's metal knee
and speed off, chasing around the square.
You think you're such a flash
with your red shirt flapping in the breeze.
Then you are long gone and I'm alone
with Endicott Johnson, his calm hand
clenched against one ringing, greenish knee.
I stroke the cold wrist of industrial man,
a chill straight through the finger bone.
One docile boy and girl kneel at his side
in shoes no mother's love could bronze so huge.
And four feet down a thickly muscled man of iron broods
on his mystical code: *Labor is Honorable.*

Here are the first uncertainties
of spring, but nothing comforts me,
gone stiff with terror, surrounded by the dead
and silent birds sleeping in the trees.
I find dark hieroglyphs on the girl's lace hem.
Have faith in the people. But where are they?
The iron boy studies his anchored shoe.
Some stranger runs maniacally at me,
mouth open in wind, hair like a nimbus
lit by the greasy streetlamp glare.
I grab at his cool, familiar hand, the streak
of red life leaping through the shadowy park.

ENDLESS LIFE

Let me lay my hand on the head of the Reaper
at the moment of death, when the curtains part
for mourners drawn to the feet of the still sleeper.

The River Styx tonight lies overlapping Baltimore,
a city langorously shining. And the body, worn
thin as a shell makes its last journey.

We the living feel the wave creep by
which carries it off. Then silence drifting,
a slow pull of darkness from below;

and faith spins out the rescuer's rope
from which we learn to hang—
till in the end the waters open.

Gathered into a knot, and flecked
with foam, loom the survivors:
the bright souls, immortal lovers.

PASSOVER

I call to warn my father, dreaming his dream
of sweet retirement five miles from Disneyworld;
mark a red *x* on the door.
Too late—my mother's gone, knocked out by sugary wine.

No one alive can say the Hebrew prayers.
I fumble with a friend on "mortar" and "plague"
till he recalls the word for grief.
We light and smoke these bitter herbs.

Elijah—Elijah—come back to the table:
sip from some drunken uncle's cup,
those pranksters stretched in gloom over the groaning
board of bones, salt water, yellow cloths.

The angel of death flies slower
in his eternal circle. Blown weakly in,
he closes the door, locks it, sits, and begins
to drain the dark wine brimming at the empty place.

MARRIED LOVE

The trees are uncurling their first
green messages: Spring, and some man
lets his arm brush my arm in a darkened
theater. Faint-headed, I fight the throb.
Later I dream
the gas attendant puts a cool hand
on my breast, asking a question.
Slowly I rise through the surface of the dream,
brushing his hand and my own heat away.

Young, I burned to marry. Married,
the smoulder goes on underground,
clutching at weeds, writhing everywhere.
I'm trying to talk to a friend on burning
issues, flaming from the feet up,
drinking in his breath, touching his wrist.
I want to grab the pretty woman
on the street, seize the falcon
by its neck, beat my way into whistling steam.

I turn to you in the dark, oh husband,
watching your lit breath circle the pillow.
Then you turn to me, throwing first one limb
and then another over me, in the easy brotherly
lust of marriage. I cling to you
as if I were a burning ship and you
could save me, as if I won't go sliding down
beneath you soon; as if our lives are made of rise
and fall, and we could ride this out forever,
with longing's thunder rolling heavy in our arms.

INTO THE TERRITORIES

Here it is again in St. Paul, Minnesota,
the international conspiracy of kindness.
I've never seen so many businessmen
stare with such humble interest at a passing girl.
The Mississippi River, conqueror at spelling bees,
smoothes like the forehead of a peaceful man,
shines broad and sleepy at the end of day.
And down the flowered streets
saunter all the other spring somnambulists
in lightweight clothing, grazing
against car bumpers, climbing catwalks
of elegance high above downtown Minneapolis,
land of cloud-tinted water.

By dark I'm at a funny farm
for businessmen; white paint, a t.v. lounge
and open phones along the corridors.
I've come here to be institutionalized
with fifty other youthful leaders of America,
paid by a foundation that stands by corn.
We sit in tiny metal chairs attached to desks
and raise our hands to suggest leadership qualities.
I am the only leader in America
who still smokes cigarettes. The others gently
wave my fiery breath away. Our lecturer drones on,
stutters on every *m*, so that I learn to dread it coming up,
the way he sticks and then goes under, like a drowning man.
But soon we all drift off, caught
in our strangeness, every one of us.
Fifty new souls rise slowly up and bow

to one another, and go their own way,
leaving the nodding heads behind.

The young doctor holds me around the waist
as we dance beneath a moon I failed to notice;
breathing at his shirt, making an effort not to sweat.
He hands me photos of his wife and three small sons
and when I show my family in return—
one dead ex-husband and a fiancé—
he gravely palms my skull of hair,
wishes me luck. Why are we dancing together
like this, why am I rigidly standing
in some physician's sweet-smelling arms?
Since both of us are leaders, neither one
follows well; the dance stumbles along.
Is something in the air of Minnesota?
The sky's so high and wide
it drives the horses wild
across the grass trying
to find the end of it.

But my whole being yearns toward the dying East.
The man who runs the candy store
gives me a chocolate pretzel, puts his arm
across my shoulders, and says he'd
ride with me to Syracuse if he wasn't
just back from New York himself. Five days
of unremitting kindness have left me trembly,
without resources, like a child.
Walking beside the tracks
I pat myself gently, checking
for missing parts—train tickets, wallet,

breastbone and ribs. Yes, here they are
again; my naming of things complete,
the week's work done,
my loneliness intact.

ELEGY FOR A BEAGLE MUTT

What a season this is:
darkness making its sure descent, the motley rose
of drooping head, and wet leaves plastered everywhere
in bright chaotic paths. My leaping pup—
she of the quick pulse coiled
on the bed who slept in outlandish,
graceful twists of the neck,
shook by the door, lay dripping on the porch,
broke the spines of rabbits and squirrels,
begged at every table, that last morning
rose from the foot of the bed
thrusting her jaw into my face to stare:
stern, puzzled, forgiving glance, crushed
under a school bus, gone.
The sprawl of bones with pomp and grief
is laid to rest beneath a rusty tree—
and still I see her low shape moving
cautiously through every raining bush
or flashing under weeds as flaps of newspaper blow by.
If I had been out walking,
if I had thrown myself into her childish play,
she who skittered and obeyed could have led me,
licking the hand of every passing soul, and pulled me
willy-nilly through the final gate. Now the corpse commands
and I stay here, reminded of the Buddhist saint
who waited at the gates of heaven
ten thousand years with his faithful dog, till both
were permitted in. Lithe dancer, I am reeling on a planet
gone to dark moods and imbalance, silent and unsafe,
imagining your collar of bones hooked small
under my fist—wait for me!

RETURN OF THE MAGI

I'm so unused to footsteps near my door I scream
when the actor downstairs scratches on my screen.
No autographs, he wisecracks, then he coughs;
he's having a little party, hopes it won't
disturb me. Of course, he adds, I'm welcome to come.

With 8 more shopping days
at 10 P.M. at 5 below
I struggle past his dark apartment, quiet as a lake;
only his droopy wreath's lit up
over the door. His cardboard sign,
a cartoon cat, says Let's Be Friends.
I'm in the kitchen, resting my feet
when far below
as if from underwater
a baritone, tenor, and bass guitar
come quavering on. Have a Merry,
Berry Christmas. Thrum!
Then Rudolph the Red-Nosed Reindeer,
thrum thrum!
After a pause, O Holy Night.
From time to time his screen door bangs
as guests escape into the cold.
Their voices dim, then flutter up like steam
till midnight when with late heat through the grate
the last trio descends on We Three Kings in harmony—
the wise men humming through the vents,
into the cracked night, whirling bits of snow.
Their voices rise up, hushed and goony.

WHAT'S IN THE AIR

It's not disaster
—something shaken from the trees
when loneliness like this comes drifting down.

I see it on faces;
a window in every house sealed blue with late t.v.
as father's car rolls like a summons through the snow.

The new rage is religion
or the blackened end of the world—our longing
to be saved becomes revenge.

Brooding or troubled spirit,
where in the world are you hiding, in what motel
of past life, keeping fresh at whose expense?

Spring bumbles in
with flowering, chilly rains bright
over the yellow wands of willows

as some man touches
his console set to let a little light in
on his gloomy gathering of chairs.

He stares into the street
and his homesick thought drums like a wave
in that sea of faith lit up above the ghostly, neon world.

ANOTHER SLEEPLESS NIGHT AMONG THE RUINS

This spring-like February evening,
pink sky shading down to lead,
I stand under clear white butterflies—
a flock of wings hung folded from the sleeping tree.
When one cloud moves they turn to stars of ice.
Ah frozen ringing street, stricken beneath my boots!

The Church of the Slow Children
has no other name, only the glowing shield
out on the road
though I circle around the gray stone
dark within its spider sprawl,
one bell and cross flung
into the highest air: steel spray
of its peculiar blossoming.

At daylight's edge
before I climb the flights
to my third floor roof of rooms
I stand like this sometimes and breathe
and count the endless movement of my breastbone heaving
while dawn glitters in like a red tide and nothing
else is there. . . .

From her corner of the sky
my steady neighbor Venus
points me up till I can see
the path of planets burn and gleam and widen out
—so like my own slow way past grief.

FOR A SLEEPING RUNNING BACK

I'd watched him hurtle past the linemen like a fist
sailing away, heard a dark thunder clap of ribs
as he danced down all along his forearms,
rose up and jogged back into place
as if he'd practiced for this
shouldering through walls.

One night he showed up, moving his elbows
close to his sides, swinging and scraping his feet,
and would not talk, or eat the candies set out in a dish
or look steadily anywhere but at the football films
in whose blue rickety blurred light
his face partway relaxed,
the Cupid's upper lip stuck hungrily
over the lower, sharp
as an aching old man's.

By midnight he was just a teenager again, seemed doomed;
brushing his teeth five times,
alone in the living room reading
slowly, feet jiggling on the sofa,
homework lit by a small lamp overhead,
the bright red flickering
heat-lightning of his radio
burning into the night.

Beneath Aunt Lucy's flowered heirloom quilt
his sleeping form rose and sank down.
The dim gray air took on his gloom, crackling electricity.
Storm-gatherer, cloud-bearer;
seeker and chaser of bad weather.
Two white gym socks, still at last,
lay spooky in a line of light that split the room.

On my side of the dark
I could recall how many afternoons
he'd rushed past young men faceless in their masks
to bring something a long way back
he cradled at his chest,
to be the leaper, hurling nowhere, risking no wings.
I held one hand out, letting his breath
curl up like smoke into my palm—
his oxygen, so clear and quick and hot,
so lonely at that altitude.

THE SPEED OF DEATH

Hermes dips his ankle wings
low to the ground, mumbling, moving faster—
his god's fist closing across the sky.
The speeding hare, the train—the bullet flash
of crashed velocity and cruising things.
I am not tired; sleep passed by.
Cold air shuts off the lights.
Your tired voice beat in my heart all night.

FINDING THE WORDS

His bare, round, sloping shoulder rose,
brightened and bent over the dog's new grave.
Maples blew up cloudy leaves, white-fluttering wind
beneath which a red sumac burned.
He raised the shovel like a sword
while I stood behind the window
watching, mouthing farewell.

Then he laid out his tools, stepped quickly
around the corner of a year and down
among cool gravestones
drizzled on, gilded as lamps at evening.
What could I do with the hair shirt of frost
he'd worn all his life
with his wintry indifference—
I was more like
the sumac weed, hotheaded
and fierce beneath sweeter fires.

It came to me in somber fall,
when he was gone
in one quick stride
to reach that window—open it, call
Come inside. You've worked enough.

THANKSGIVING

The deer are just thankful it's over—
whole herds of them, grins sagging upside down,
stretched out on racks of wagons and trucks
huffing along Route 17 at dusk, in snow.
On vans, a few early Christmas trees strapped down.

Main Street at twilight is a skating rink
the adults maneuver down with dignity
clutching groceries, treading ice,
their arms filling with sleet.
But when the children are in bed,
uncles and aunts asleep
beside the fizzing t.v. set,
a drunk picks his slow way downtown.
He slides into the Donut Shoppe
and sips black coffee, his face an inch
above the cup. He eats
with two or three aproned bodies near.

And yes, beloved, you're right,
he's grateful
for the overhead pink
fluorescent lights, the sugary taste,
and all the gathered company.

WEARING HIS OLD BOOTS

If I pull on two pairs of woolen socks I can
step into his boots, but never
dance the bearish dance
that sent him rolling to the edges
of his dainty farmer's foot.

With me there is no shining
from the ankle to a helmet of light
colored hair by which lost moviegoers
found their seats back in the dark.
I can only heave my broken,
black-haired cry.
I can never be that one I loved.

His feet in cold clay are too heavy to lift
so I stumble along, led by
the bulging toe of his sad genius,
the blue veined foot
which moved in time to the life
that blew through him.

I'd like to stop on my own
two knees and stand on them awhile.
As in the old days, he grips
my shin, pitching me forward.
No, but . . . No, but . . .
The ground is cracking everywhere.
In clodhopper boots he holds me up.

AT THE COMMON TABLE

I stare into the glass-paned kitchen door
and see a slight girl stuffing fruitcake
in her mouth. She jerks with fright.
I lean over a tin of World Famous Fruitcake
and the world leans out:
A woman eats from her cupped hand, over the sink
while far away in wonder the aging boy
who axe-murdered his father slowly reads directions,
"Use sharp knife and wipe blade
after each slice, never 'saw' your cake."
And the famous who gave their tributes
rattle the cupboards for one last crumb,
their bloodstreams hungry for the fast delivery.
You could get sick from this feast, and you do,
but there's no stopping, you crave and devour,
you eat and your gorge rises higher.
You're finally sharing the worldwide body,
ashes you never guessed would taste so good.

THE MOURNER'S CHRISTMAS

I've waited a long while in this antique snow light
staring out onto the cold approach of Christmas morning.
Nothing but the flakes of shadows falling
across the blue-white snow, the *chuff chuff chuff* fright
of a lone car listing downtown, adrift like a ghostly boat.

Inside, white stars are blinking on my tree
and last year's ornaments dangle above the gifts
stretched in a gold- and silver-papered river
along the shifting floor. In this magical twilight
I believe I'll find you, your hand out for my ankle bone.

A cracked melodious French horn is ringing
its call through every room, but the angel atop
the high branch lifts a mute gold bell, her lips are stopped
and still I stumble through the dark halls singing
till I hit the far side of forgetfulness.

I will lighten up from foot to skull,
my breastbone pricked with nervous flame
and needles of ash bear me away.
Meanwhile I burn to get my fill.
I stand in the light to let the morning in.

THE ACCIDENT

This is the young man, two cars ahead
who skidded across a double yellow line
and tumbled off his bike to lie with bent legs crossed
odd as a praying mantis or a fallen deer.

Young man, with your scruffy jeans, the sad dirt
brownish-gray and permanently poor, the black helmet
over your head, your gashed brow and the pool of crimson blood—
when they stripped away your shirt your chest had a thin
bone-china pallor, and when I walked close your fierce eyes
were rolled up like a dead gangster's or saint's, scorning the joke
till your pool of dark blood
ran toward my feet and chased me away.

Emmerich, rising toward heaven, Emmerich
already gone, hearing the scorched flare
struck and lit ten feet away,
feeling the blonde hysterical woman near,
the realtor who trembled violently but squatted
behind you gripping your helmet so your neck
could not roll back, her fingers splayed in terror,
red with blood she would not wipe off—
the drugged brown aura of hypnosis over it all.
Such chaos and collapsing of the earth's noises in you—
the dismal gathering and sirens collecting for the kill
one after another, blocked traffic, and you still
lying with your legs oddly crossed, your dirty boots,
the breath of life leaving through one crushed rib.

This is how you pushed
through your wife's smooth legs, your beer-breath fired
with sweetness and desire; your two jobs,
daylight time at E-Z Motors, and evenings, manager

at Bobby Dee's, that famous, noisy, hot, beer-brawling place.
Here lies your fine talent with machines,
the way your silky skin would soak up black oil,
and long days at the beach, the scratchy blanket,
the long smooth waves, your body hard
against a pillow age 13.
These are your bony knees, your broken tooth,
your straight brown hair
which the sunlight wore transfixed like a gold crown.

Emmerich Antoni, I prayed for you to rise
on your twisted feet, and hobble away like a bumped deer,
Emmerich Antoni, you lay there thinking nothing,
thinking black thoughts, thinking about your last meal,
about your first girl, your young wife,
thinking about your mother grieving—
Already with her as she studies the grass before your grave,
already reading the paper and the fine print,
sitting around the shaky kitchen table with your wife Regina
and all her brothers and sisters and the covered dishes they bring.
Say goodbye to your mother, who packed you off to school
with bent bologna sandwich, pickle and orange dew.
To your father, in another country now,
but who hears you call, and startled, looks up to see you pass.
Goodbye to your sisters, the lovely and the noisy one.
To your bosses, who will grimly hear the news.
Lean close to Regina's curving neck; farewell.

You are doing what you have to do; the earth's lamps
are turned down to twilight blue, you are sinking,
finding your way out and holding your breath, it's
easy, easy, the man in a blue shirt kneels in the road

and pumps your chest, the woman who held your head is gone.
Young man, with your neck so oddly thrown, and your broken leg
tossed over the other, with your long foot elegantly slanting down,
I was your guardian angel, I wasn't looking, I was busy praying,
and stepped back at the sight of your saintly dirty face,
your little collection of purplish blood, I was the one
moaning Breathe! Breathe! long after you'd come and gone
—and no one said, You are still you but changing fast.
We are taking you to the hospital, now we are lifting you,
It doesn't hurt, The traffic is stopped, It is September 30
1983, In America which recedes beneath you Emmerich Antoni

sailing over the horizon of lost time.
Forgive my cowardice at the guardrail, and my self-pity.
You were on your way home; you slammed
into another car and flew; no one is hurt
but you. You sleep, but your spirit buzzes incandescently.
Something in you keeps flying, coming along
under the wing of the horse chestnut tree
at the corner of Conklin and the Exchange Street Bridge,
where the angel waits for you, gunning his engine—
under that fast blazing canopy
signal left in the green shade and go home.

PITT POETRY SERIES

Ed Ochester, General Editor

Dannie Abse, *Collected Poems*
Claribel Alegría, *Flowers from the Volcano*
Jon Anderson, *Death and Friends*
Jon Anderson, *In Sepia*
Jon Anderson, *Looking for Jonathan*
John Balaban, *After Our War*
Michael Benedikt, *The Badminton at Great Barrington; Or, Gustave Mahler & the Chattanooga Choo-Choo*
Michael Burkard, *Ruby for Grief*
Kathy Callaway, *Heart of the Garfish*
Siv Cedering, *Letters from the Floating World*
Lorna Dee Cervantes, *Emplumada*
Robert Coles, *A Festering Sweetness: Poems of American People*
Leo Connellan, *First Selected Poems*
Kate Daniels, *The White Wave*
Norman Dubie, *Alehouse Sonnets*
Stuart Dybek, *Brass Knuckles*
Odysseus Elytis, *The Axion Esti*
John Engels, *Blood Mountain*
Brendan Galvin, *The Minutes No One Owns*
Brendan Galvin, *No Time for Good Reasons*
Gary Gildner, *Blue Like the Heavens: New & Selected Poems*
Gary Gildner, *Digging for Indians*
Gary Gildner, *First Practice*
Gary Gildner, *Nails*
Gary Gildner, *The Runner*
Bruce Guernsey, *January Thaw*
Mark Halperin, *Backroads*
Michael S. Harper, *Song: I Want a Witness*
John Hart, *The Climbers*
Gwen Head, *Special Effects*
Gwen Head, *The Ten Thousandth Night*
Barbara Helfgott Hyett, *In Evidence: Poems of the Liberation of Nazi Concentration Camps*
Milne Holton and Graham W. Reid, eds., *Reading the Ashes: An Anthology of the Poetry of Modern Macedonia*
Milne Holton and Paul Vangelisti, eds., *The New Polish Poetry: A Bilingual Collection*
David Huddle, *Paper Boy*
Lawrence Joseph, *Shouting at No One*

Shirley Kaufman, *From One Life to Another*
Shirley Kaufman, *Gold Country*
Ted Kooser, *One World at a Time*
Ted Kooser, *Sure Signs: New and Selected Poems*
Larry Levis, *Winter Stars*
Larry Levis, *Wrecking Crew*
Robert Louthan, *Living in Code*
Tom Lowenstein, tr., *Eskimo Poems from Canada and Greenland*
Archibald MacLeish, *The Great American Fourth of July Parade*
Peter Meinke, *Trying to Surprise God*
Judith Minty, *In the Presence of Mothers*
Carol Muske, *Camouflage*
Carol Muske, *Wyndmere*
Leonard Nathan, *Carrying On: New & Selected Poems*
Leonard Nathan, *Dear Blood*
Leonard Nathan, *Holding Patterns*
Kathleen Norris, *The Middle of the World*
Sharon Olds, *Satan Says*
Greg Pape, *Black Branches*
Greg Pape, *Border Crossings*
James Reiss, *Express*
Ed Roberson, *Etai-Eken*
William Pitt Root, *Faultdancing*
Liz Rosenberg, *The Fire Music*
Eugene Ruggles, *The Lifeguard in the Snow*
Dennis Scott, *Uncle Time*
Herbert Scott, *Groceries*
Richard Shelton, *Of All the Dirty Words*
Richard Shelton, *Selected Poems, 1969-1981*
Richard Shelton, *You Can't Have Everything*
Arthur Smith, *Elegy on Independence Day*
Gary Soto, *Black Hair*
Gary Soto, *The Elements of San Joaquin*
Gary Soto, *The Tale of Sunlight*
Gary Soto, *Where Sparrows Work Hard*
Tomas Tranströmer, *Windows & Stones: Selected Poems*
Chase Twichell, *Northern Spy*
Chase Twichell, *The Odds*
Constance Urdang, *The Lone Woman and Others*
Constance Urdang, *Only the World*
Ronald Wallace, *Tunes for Bears to Dance To*
Cary Waterman, *The Salamander Migration and Other Poems*
Bruce Weigl, *A Romance*
David P. Young, *The Names of a Hare in English*
Paul Zimmer, *Family Reunion: Selected and New Poems*